Custom Tumbler Business

Sell Beautifully Designed Cups and Watch the Money Pour In

Elsie Doyle

By reading this notice, the reader agrees that under no circumstances is the author responsible for any losses, direct or indirect, that are incurred as a result of the use of information contained within this book, including, but not limited to, errors, omissions, or inaccuracies.

Table of Contents

Introduction

What's one of the most popular items right now? It would of course have to be a tumbler! People carry these around with them everywhere they go. People need to stay hydrated so carrying around something that gives you constant access to water makes sense.

However, cups are so much more than that as you'll soon find out. It's about more than just trying to stay hydrated. In fact, I would say people buy tumblers for plenty of reasons other than the main practical one.

With that being said, this gives you an opportunity to capitalize on the momentum from this product. This product has a practical reason for people to buy it, but it also has social reasons as well. This creates a powerful effect especially when we're talking about custom tumblers that you can't get just anywhere.

People will want to know where that person got their tumbler from and it can create a snowball effect rather quickly. There's a lot that goes into creating a successful business of any kind, let alone a custom tumbler business. Luckily for you, you'll have the knowledge you need by reading this book. So let's go ahead and begin shall we?

Chapter 1: What Supplies Will You Need?

In order to start any business with physical products involved, you're going to need materials. The good news about this business is that yes it will cost a decent amount of money to get started, but it will be far less than a lot of other businesses out there that you could start. Before we get into supplies though, it's important to think about why you should start this business in the first place.

People Don't Stop With Just One

The first reason why selling custom tumblers is a win is because people don't buy just one. People will end up with multiple cups for better or worse. It's not unreasonable for someone to have 10 cups or more as they tend to accumulate over time for one reason or another.

Maybe someone gets a 20 oz and then they decide they want a 40 oz. Then they want one in a different color or one with a handle. Then a new cup comes out that all of their friends are getting so they get one as well.

Then they get one as a company Christmas gift and another one as a gift for Christmas. So as you can see, when people are buying tumblers, it's easy for these things to accumulate quickly. I even had one person tell me that one of her friends bought different colored cups to match her outfits for work throughout the week.

And when it comes to custom tumblers, there really is no limit. There's an endless amount of possibilities when it comes to colors, text, and pictures that a cup could be customized with, which makes it easy for the same person to buy from you multiple times. Maybe you yourself have multiple tumblers and you don't even know how you ended up with as many as you did.

Cups Are About Way More Than Practicality

Yes, drinking water and staying hydrated is an essential part of life, so there's no doubt that there's a practical reason to buy a tumbler. However, I would argue that in many cases people aren't buying cups for practical purposes.

How else can someone justify owning so many of the same item?

You see, cups are not just cups, they are accessories. Just like jewelry to help make an outfit pop, tumblers can serve the same purpose. Think back to the example I gave where someone bought different colored tumblers to match her outfits for work.

At that point, it's not about practical use, it's about making a fashion statement, and the cup becomes an extension of the person. Tumblers are also very trendy. When people's friends start to buy a product and talk about it, it can gain a ton of steam quickly.

It will make people want what their friends have. And the thing is that it's not just for adults. My 3 nieces all have tumblers and they're drinking more water because of it!

So needless to say, there's a huge opportunity here because tumblers represent who someone is. If you make someone a custom tumbler with a picture of their child on it, you bet they'll be excited to show it off!

Creative Business Where You Get to Work With Your Hands

I don't know about you, but I don't like doing desk work all day long. I want to change things up and this business allows you to do just that. I also love that I get to bring people's creations to life.

To be able to take an idea that's in someone else's head and put it on a tumbler is a truly amazing feeling and it's one that you'll get to experience regularly by being a part of this business.

Get Started With These Essentials

The following are the basics I would look into purchasing to start this business. Sure some things will vary depending on how you want to go about making your tumblers, but this is going to be a solid list to help you get started:

Tumblers

You have to buy tumblers in order to have a custom tumbler business, that's obvious. What's not so obvious is where you should buy your tumblers from. The best idea is to buy your tumblers in bulk so that way you're getting the best price per unit.

You may be hesitant at the idea of doing this, but you can buy in different quantities to help accommodate your starting budget. Even if you're brand new to this and you've never made a custom tumbler before, it's still a good idea to buy some tumblers so that you can get some practice in.

When you're just beginning, you can buy in smaller quantities and then buy in bulk sizes once you have more orders coming in. So where should you buy your tumblers from? You do have a few options to choose from luckily. The following are all good options that are worth looking into:

-MakerFlo Crafts
-Heat Press Nation
-The Stainless Depot

CrystalLac or Epoxy

You need a product that will allow your tumblers to have a smooth finish and allow something such as glitter to adhere to your cup. Without the use of a product such as epoxy, your end product isn't going to turn out too well. Glitter will be coming off of your cups and they'll have that gritty texture because the glitter itself will be the outermost layer.

By using epoxy, you'll be able to create a glossy outside layer on your cups to lock inner layers, such as glitter, in place. Some people don't like to use epoxy because of some of the chemicals that it uses, so people like to use a product known as CrystalLac as an alternative. Both of these products serve the same purpose, so it really comes down to personal preference for what you want to use!

Cup Turner

If you've never heard of a cup turner before, imagine a device with poles that you put your cups in that will continually spin your cups in a clockwise motion. This product does exactly what it sounds like, which is to spin cups. So what's so important about spinning cups? Well, there are a couple of reasons for it.

The first is that it will make your life a lot easier when you're applying your epoxy to your cup. The same thing goes for applying dyes or glitter. It will also come in handy once you're waiting for your epoxy to cure as you want to keep your cup moving during this process.

Cutting Machine

A cutting machine allows you to cut out precise fonts and texts straight from your computer. If you're going to be adding text to your tumblers, then buying a cutting machine from Cricut or Silhouette America is worth looking into. These machines are going to cost you a good bit of money, somewhere in the realm of $300 depending on which one you go with.

So consider buying used if you need to save money, or you can hold off and not use text as an option for your customization until you're able to save up enough money to buy one of these machines. Sure you could do things manually by printing off the text you need and cutting it out, but it's really hard to be precise, especially when you're working with tricky fonts. It's far easier to be able to use a machine that can cut things out exactly how you need it to be.

Glitter

Glitter is one of the different types of materials that you can use as part of your designs. This is how you can create really cool and sparkly designs using multiple different colors or fading looks.

Rhinestones

Just like with glitter you can use rhinestones as another item to help create your custom designs. You can create a custom tumbler purely using rhinestones or you can use them in combination with other materials like glitter, dye, text, or pictures. For instance, a customer might want a custom design that involves a picture. You could use rhinestones to outline the border of the picture to really make it pop.

Tumbler Heat Press

A tumbler heat press is something you can use for creating sublimation designs. It's not necessary and it depends on what kind of tumbler you want to make. Essentially, sublimation uses a combination of gas and heat to embed an image onto a cup.

So when a cup has a sticker on it, you can tell that there's an additional layer to the cup and over time it will start to scrape off if an additional layer of epoxy is not applied afterwards. With sublimation, the image becomes a part of the cup itself so you don't have to worry about the image getting dinged up over time, and it also creates a cleaner look.

Latex Gloves

Making custom tumblers is a messy process. You're dealing with things like epoxy which can irritate some people's skin and glitter is messy as well. This is why you'll want to invest in some disposable gloves that you can use while you're working. Some people prefer to use their hands when they're applying epoxy while others will use a brush. The preference is up to you, but either way, it's best to be smart and wear gloves to ensure your hands stay protected.

Plastic Measuring Cups

Epoxy comes in two parts, part A and part B. Part of the process of using epoxy involves mixing equal parts of A and B together. It's very important to ensure that you're mixing equal parts together, so this is where measuring cups come into play. The reason why you'll want to use plastic cups is so that you can dispose of them once you're done using them. It's not worth the hassle of trying to clean out your measuring cups to try and reuse them.

Stirring Sticks

Once you combine part A and part B of your epoxy, you'll need to use something to stir them that's cheap and disposable, so this is why wooden stirring sticks are my preferred choice here. Anything that you can use to stir something with that you are comfortable disposing afterwards will work just fine though.

Spray Paint

Pretty much any tumbler you buy in bulk is going to be white. You might want the base color of your tumbler to be something other than white, which is why spray paint is needed. Let's say you're making a cup where you plan on covering the entire surface in pink glitter.

You'll still want to spray paint the cup pink first before you apply the glitter to ensure that if there are empty spots with the glitter, they'll be pink and not white, which will throw off the look of your cup.

Vinyl for Custom Words

When you're making custom words for your tumbler, you don't use regular printer paper as this will make your tumbler look like a cheap product when we want things to look top-notch.

Instead, you want to use vinyl and you can buy vinyl from whatever brand you bought your cutting machine from. Vinyl also comes in a variety of different colors, which allows you to get the perfect look instead of being stuck with using something like a standard white color all of the time.

Water Slide Paper

Using water slide paper is an alternative to using a sublimation heat press to apply a picture to a tumbler. Essentially, you'll buy a special type of paper known as water slide paper. You'll print off the image you want to put on the cup, you'll submerge the image in water, then place it on the cup, and then remove the backing. It's a simple process and it's a cheaper alternative to sublimation.

Alcohol Dye

Dye is another way that you can customize your tumblers. Alcohol dye, just like glitter or spray, doesn't necessarily have to be used, it all depends on the type of look you want to create. I do recommend using different materials so that you can be versatile and meet any customer request that comes your way.

Alcohol dye is another reason why you'll want a cup turner as it will make the process of applying your alcohol dye much smoother. You can buy this in a wide variety of different colors so there's a lot of possibilities for what you can create.

Printer

The kind of printer that you buy doesn't really matter, in fact, you can probably use a printer that you already have at home. Depending on the design you're looking to create, you may not even need a printer, but you will need one for printing off images on your sublimation paper and water slide paper.

Heat Gun

A heat gun is used to help pop any bubbles that form once the epoxy is applied. One key thing to note is that you want to continually move your heat gun and don't let it stay on one area of your tumbler for too long. Doing so can burn through your layer of epoxy and defeat what you were trying to accomplish in the first place.

Rubbing alcohol

Sometimes you may end up getting paint or something else on the inside of the rim when you're creating your tumbler. You'll definitely want to remove anything that gets inside of the rim as this will create immediate distrust with your customer.

They'll be uncertain if it's even safe to drink from the cup. So be sure to use some rubbing alcohol to clean the inside of the rim just in case some of your materials get into an area it's not supposed to.

Respirator

When you're dealing with epoxy, the smell can be very strong, so it's a good idea to wear a respirator so that you're not potentially breathing in any chemicals from the epoxy.

Chapter 2: Process to Make a Custom Tumbler

In this chapter, I'm going to go over the process for how you can make a custom tumbler. Please note that this is one way of going about things and not the only way.

The process can also vary depending on what type of materials and supplies you're using. For the sake of this chapter, I'm going to be going over the process for making a glitter cup using epoxy.

Step 1: Preparation

The first thing that you want to do is get everything prepared. You want to go ahead and put your gloves on, and then prep the tumbler you're going to be customizing by wiping it down with an alcohol pad. This will help to ensure you're working with a clean surface and that the materials you're applying to your cup will adhere better to it.

Step 2: Spray Paint

If you're looking to have the base of your cup be a certain color other than white, this is the part of the process where you're going to want to spray paint your cup. For example, maybe you want a black base with gold glitter. You're already going to want to spray paint the cup black this early in the process.

A couple of tips when you're spray painting is to ensure that the cup is upside down to help prevent paint from getting on the inside rim of your cup. You'll want to use a stick that will allow you to hold the cup out and away from you while keeping the cup in the upside-down position. If spray paint does get on the inside of your rim, you can always scrap it off afterwards using something like sandpaper.

The next thing you'll want to do is make sure that you're not continuously holding down the trigger on the spray paint can. Doing this can cause paint to run down the sides and can create a sloppy look.

Instead, you want to spray in bursts where you press down and then release. Then you'll turn the cup and press down to spray a new area of the cup to ensure you're not double-coating one area before other areas are covered.

Step 3: Prep Your Epoxy

Now it's time to prep your epoxy. Epoxy comes with a part A and a part B. You'll need to mix them together by pouring equal amounts of part A and part B into separate measuring cups. Once you have equal amounts of both, you can pour them together and stir.

You now have some ready-to-use epoxy. It's important to note that you don't want to mix your epoxy parts together crazy fast. Instead, go slowly, and once you're ready, you can start to apply the epoxy to your cup.

You'll want to make sure that your tumbler is in your cup turner and is spinning. Then you can use your hands (with gloves on) or a brush to steadily apply the epoxy to your cup as it's spinning.

You'll want to ensure that you apply epoxy evenly to your whole cup. Once you've done this, it's time to move to the next step.

Step 4: Use Your Heat Gun

After applying your epoxy, you're likely going to notice that some bubbles have formed on your cup. Leaving these bubbles will not create a good look for your customer, so now is the time to remove them with your heat gun. The number one thing to remember here is to keep it moving with your heat gun or else you'll run the risk of burning right through the layer of epoxy that you just put on your cup.

Step 5: Apply Your Glitter

Now you have prepared your cup and it's ready for glitter to be applied. You have a foundation that your glitter can stick to with ease. You'll want to ensure that your tumbler is still on the cup turner as this will be the easier way to apply your glitter.

I believe the best way to apply your glitter is in a parallel fashion to the direction the cup is spinning rather than perpendicular to the way the cup is spinning. Applying glitter in a parallel direction will make it much more seamless if you're looking to apply multiple different kinds of glitter to your tumbler.

For example, let's say you want to cover the top half in pink glitter and the bottom half in red glitter. By applying the glitter in a parallel manner, you'll have a much easier time stopping at the halfway point and keeping an even layer at the bottom before the next color starts.

Step 6: Wait and Apply More Epoxy

The next part isn't exactly fun because who likes to wait? But you need to give your glitter some time to fully adhere to your cup before you do anything else. If you immediately try and apply your next layer of epoxy, then your glitter is going to be sliding around and creating a frustrating time for you and a cup with patches of no glitter.

So once you apply your glitter, you'll want to wait for 4 hours. Then once that time has passed, you're now ready to apply your next layer of epoxy. This layer of epoxy will help to give your tumbler a smooth surface.

Once this layer has been applied, you'll want to leave your tumbler spinning on your cup turner for 24 hours so that your epoxy can fully cure. Once 24 hours have passed, you're now ready to apply the finishing touches to your cup.

Step 7: Smooth Out Your Cup

To finish up your cup, you're going to want to use a high grain sandpaper to smooth out any rough spots that have appeared on your cup. It's best to be gentle with your sandpaper and go slow and then put more force into it as needed to smooth out any rough spots. Approaching things in this manner will ensure that you don't push things too far and sand through your top layer of epoxy.

If you do happen to go too deep, you can always apply more epoxy in that area and let it cure again. You'll also want to smooth out the top rim of the cup to ensure that it's smooth and to help create a clean look. Once you have sanded the cup, you'll then want to go over it with another alcohol prep pad to ensure the cup is clean.

Now at this point your cup could be considered done or you might want to add some additional things to your cup such as pictures or text. If this is a cup design where you're going to be adding these types of things to your tumbler, then continue to the next step.

Step 8: Apply Images and Text as Needed

This is where you'll want to apply any sort of pictures or text to your cup if this is part of the design for your cup. If you have a cutting machine, applying text to your cup will be super seamless. You'll simply have the machine cut out the words you need and you can peel off the backing and apply it like a sticker.

For adding a picture, I recommend using water slide paper like I mentioned earlier. The process is pretty straightforward once you've printed off the image.

After the image has been in water, you can place it where you want it to be on the cup and then peel off the back layer, and boom your cup now has a picture on it. At this point, you could leave your cup as is and there wouldn't be anything wrong with that, but the next step would be a good one to take.

Step 9: Apply a Final Layer of Epoxy

If you decide to skip this step, your images and text will still be secure on the cup. However, over time the vinyl and image can start to chip away and it will look less than ideal as time goes on. To prevent this from happening, you can apply another layer of epoxy to your cup and now any images or text that you've added in will be sealed in just like the glitter.

Your cup will have a smooth and glossy look with no bumps where the text or image is. Once you've applied your final layer of epoxy, you'll want to go over it with the sandpaper and an alcohol pad like I mentioned before to ensure that you get rid of any rough spots on the cup.

You only need to apply sandpaper to the last epoxy layer of your cup because it doesn't matter if the base layers feel smooth. Then be sure to wait 24 hours to let it fully cure, and you only need to wait 4 hours in between applying base layers. As long as you're removing bubbles from each layer using your heat gun you'll be good because you don't want any bubbles on a base epoxy layer messing up the aesthetic of your cup.

Once you've completed this step go ahead and congratulate yourself because you've completed your custom cup! After the epoxy has fully cured, you'll now be ready to ship off or deliver the cup to the customer. Also if you don't want to use epoxy, you can use Crystal Lac instead to achieve a similar result.

What About Sublimation?

You might also be interested in making custom tumblers via sublimation, so I want to cover that process as well. Essentially you're going to need a tumbler heat press and sublimation paper. You'll print off the image you're going to use and then on your heat press, you'll set the temperature and duration accordingly depending on the size of the cup.

Your machine will give you these guidelines. You'll then want to wrap the image around your cup and use heat tape to hold it in place. Next, put the cup inside the press, press the start button, and let the machine work its magic.

Once it's finished, rotate the cup and repeat the process if the image is going to completely surround the cup. That's all there is to the process, so it's rather simple.

Some people will put their tumblers in a shrink wrap sleeve as they believe that this helps the image come out looking better on the other side. I don't believe that this is a requirement by any means, but it's something you can test out and see if you get better results with.

Lastly, one piece of advice I'd like to leave you with before moving onto the next chapter is to not be afraid to practice before you profit. Your first customers are going to be critical to your success and you'll want them to be very satisfied with their tumbler. This will lead to positive reviews and them being eager to show off their tumbler to their friends.

In order to reach that point though, you will have to invest some time and money into practicing the art of making custom tumblers. You're going to make mistakes and things won't be perfect. That's totally okay!

It's better to learn when there's no pressure rather than to get frustrated when you're making a cup for a customer. So don't be afraid to practice to get your feet wet and gain the skills you need to be successful with this business!

Chapter 3: What to Charge

This is going to be my favorite chapter to write in the entire book because I believe that it's the most important. Yes, you read that right! You can make the best custom tumblers out there.

You can have the best marketing ability, but if your pricing is off, then you're going to be wasting your time. As you're about to learn, many people get it wrong when it comes to pricing products simply because of their own limiting beliefs. You have to overcome any doubts or worries that you may have in regards to your pricing if you want this business to truly change your life like it has the capabilities of doing.

Do You Want to Own Your Job or Run a Business?

I want to start off by asking a question that will set the framework for everything else in this chapter. That question is, do you want to own your job or run a business? This is something you may not have even thought about, so what does it mean to own your job?

Well at a typical job, you'll trade hours for dollars. So if you make $25 an hour then that's what you'll make for every hour that you're on the job. When you start your own business, you're going to be doing everything yourself, and oftentimes people end up trapped where they find themselves doing more work for what turns out to be a lower hourly wage than if they were to work a job.

However, the difference is that you at least get to be your own boss, so that's a plus. But the reality for a lot of small business owners is that they're never able to get themselves to a place where their business gives them true freedom. I'm talking about where they can make more money from having to do less work.

That of course doesn't happen right away, it takes time, but pricing is a big hurdle that will keep you trapped. By pricing your products low you're setting yourself up to continue to own your job. Think about it, if your prices are low, then you're not going to be profiting enough to bring on additional help that can allow you to have more free time.

If you want to bring on additional labor, then your production costs are going to increase and therefore your prices are going to have to reflect that. So when you're starting out, being diligent with your pricing is key to succeeding. So how should you price your custom tumblers?

How Should You Price Your Custom Tumblers?

Okay so let's get into the meat of this chapter. For many people when they start this type of business, they'll talk themselves out of what they should charge and they'll settle. They'll doubt that anyone would ever want to buy a tumbler for that much money so they lower their prices to the point where they grow to resent their business over time.

So what's a price point that feels like a good idea, but is actually a mistake in reality? It's going to be in the $20 realm. At this price point, you're putting so much work into making the cup and marketing it, let alone your cost of goods and shipping costs, that by the time you sell a cup for $20, you're not making any real life-changing profit.

In fact, I'd argue that you're not making any profit at all. Let's say your cost of goods is $8 and your shipping cost is $8. That's already $16 without even factoring in the time it's going to take for you to make the cup.

So are you really going to be happy with $4 for all of your effort? And this is without additional help, which at this margin, you'd have no room to bring on anybody to help you out. Again this is a comfortable price point and it's easy to justify, but that has more to do with a lack of confidence in your abilities and what you're selling compared to what people are willing to pay.

A much better price point to start at is $30 per tumbler and you can build on your price from there if you want. I want you to understand though that selling your custom tumblers for $40 is very possible and this is the ideal price range that you should be aiming to sell your cups for, especially if you decide to add hired help into the mix.

Companies have been selling tumblers that aren't even customized for $40-$45 for years now and people continue to buy them without thinking twice about it. You're selling something that is unique that only you can create. Someone can't go buy a tumbler with their name or a family photo on it at the store.

They need you to make this cup a reality. Remember, a tumbler is more than something you drink a beverage from. It's an accessory that people want to show off.

Would people rather show off something unique that no one else has or something generic? The answer is obvious and even if you don't have a big brand, it doesn't matter because you have the ability to create something special that will hold sentimental value to the customer, which is what you can use to help justify a high-end price point just like a company with a big brand.

Charging Too Little Will Lead to Burnout

Burnout is a word that we hear often, but we don't think about what it's like until we're going through it. Burnout is when you continue to do something where the reward is not great enough for what you're doing. So if you had a boring job and you were making minimum wage, then you'd be much more likely to experience burnout compared to if you were working that same job and making 6 figures.

Sure you might not like it in either case, but at least in the second scenario, you're getting paid well enough for it to be worth your time. Hopefully you'll enjoy making cups enough that you won't have the experience of burnout, but it can still be something that happens to you even if you do enjoy the process. The main way you'll start to feel burnt out from this business is when you feel like you're just spinning your wheels.

You're doing all of this work, and yet you barely have anything to show for it. I'm sure you know that the majority of businesses end up failing. Something that most people don't think about though is that a business could fail simply because it wasn't worth operating anymore.

Someone might want to shut their business down and go back to a 9-5 because they'll be able to work less and still make the same amount of money or possibly even more. I don't want you to get to a point in your business where you feel like you're better off without it. If you're selling cups like crazy at a low price, sure at first you'll be excited because it feels good when others buy what we've created.

Other times though, things will start to feel like a chore. On the other hand, if our marketing efforts are off and we're unable to demonstrate the offering correctly, no sales will be made at all and this can leave you with a similar feeling.

Therefore, it's not a bad idea to strike a balance with your pricing in the beginning so that way when you do make a sale, you have something you can actually get excited over. However, you don't want to stick with your initial pricing forever, you'll need to ramp things up at a certain point. And that's what I'm about to share with you.

When Should You Increase Your Prices?

So let's say you start off by charging $30 per cup, when you should consider increasing that price? Well, the first thing you need to determine is if you are ready for a price increase of any kind. The way that you'll be able to discern this is by looking at the number of orders you are getting.

Is your business currently not selling any cups? Do you only sell a cup here and there? Or are you so busy that you can't keep up with the demand?

If you're not selling any tumblers or barely any at all, then increasing price isn't something that you should be focused on right now. Instead, you need to focus more of your attention on your ability to sell more tumblers. The way that you sell more tumblers is by getting more creative with how you promote your business.

What you don't want to do is just assume that people aren't buying because of the price and then lower your prices. This will make it more likely for you to stick with your newer low price for the long term. Meanwhile, if you never change anything with how you market your company, then that issue will still remain.

So in the future, if you do decide to raise your prices, you're going to get stuck again because you never fixed the real issue in the first place. If you are selling so many cups that you're struggling to keep up with the demand, then it's time to increase your prices. This is something that you can do gradually, such as going from $30 per tumbler to $32 per tumbler.

And then in another 60-90 days you could go from $32 to $35, or you could jump straight up to $35 or even $40. When you do increase your prices, you'll want to pay close attention to your demand. Have sales completely plummeted?

Has demand gone down slightly or have things remained about the same as they were before? If your sales have only gone down slightly or none at all, then congratulate yourself because the market was willing to pay a higher price point for your tumblers. You'll now be able to make more profit from each cup that you sell.

Even if the overall number of tumblers that you're selling per month has decreased, this isn't necessarily something to worry about. Remember, with your higher price point, you're going to be making more money from each cup that you do sell. So you're still making more money from less work.

Chapter 4: How to Promote Your Cups

As I've been alluding to throughout this book, how you promote, position, and market yourself is critical to your success at the end of the day. You can be the most skilled person there is when it comes to making custom tumblers, but your business will still fail if you're not able to properly demonstrate your value to the market.

This first starts with getting clear on who it is that you want to sell to. By getting clear on this, you'll know what message you need to convey with your marketing efforts. Then I'll cover the most effective strategies for promoting your business so that you're not wasting any time and the orders can start flowing in.

Who Do You Want to Sell Tumblers To?

Before you start marketing your business, you need to think about who it is that you want to buy your product. You might think that the answer is that you'd be happy for anyone to buy from you. Yes, this is definitely true, but when it comes to your marketing messages, you want to be speaking with one type of person in mind.

If you speak with the masses in mind, your message will fall flat because it won't appeal to anyone specifically. For instance, generally speaking, how you would get a man to be interested in buying a custom cup from you is going to be different from how you would appeal to a woman who wants to buy a cup. Men are going to be interested in different colors and they're typically not going to care for glittery and sparkly cups.

So if you're posting pictures of cute glittery cups but primarily trying to sell to men, then things aren't going to work out so well for you. It's better to create an avatar of who you think is the ideal type of person to buy the type of custom cup that you like to make. For instance, maybe you want to appeal to moms and you can create cups with family photos or with text so that someone could easily envision what their cup would look like with their children's names on it and a family photo.

Now in your marketing messages, you can speak directly to this type of person. Let's say you're making a video showing off one of your cups, you could say something such as, "If you're a mom, you work hard for your family and what I love about this type of design is that you'll have a family photo on your tumbler that's with you everywhere you go to serve as a constant reminder of what your why is."

Or you could say, "The thing I love about making tumblers is getting stopped by people who ask me where I got that cup. It's such a good feeling because these are unique items that you can't get just anywhere." The main point here is that by taking some time to think about who your ideal customer is, you can increase the likelihood of a sale happening because you're speaking directly to what it is they're already thinking about.

Position Yourself Correctly

A cup is just a cup. A pair of shoes is just a pair of shoes. Sunglasses are just sunglasses. All of these items have a basic function that they serve and yet some companies charge way more for a pair of shoes, for example, than another company does.

So even though they might have the same function, people are still willing to pay significantly more for the same item. So why would someone pay hundreds more for a pair of shoes if they're not functionally any different? It can come down to a lot of different factors, but one of them has to do with branding.

Certain brands market and position themselves as a high-end brand. So if someone is sporting around clothing from a high-end brand it makes someone feel like they are of a higher status. Another aspect of brands, high-end or not, is the social aspect.

If someone's friends are all buying a certain product, it's going to heavily influence that person to want to buy that product as well. So I'm not saying that you need to try and position your company as some high-end brand. Rather, it's important to remind yourself that people buy items for more than just practical reasons.

Therefore, you want to make sure in your marketing efforts that you speak less about the practical side of things with your product, such as how much water your cups hold or how long they keep water cold for. Yes, talk about those things sparingly, but those aren't going to be the reasons why someone is going to want to buy a cup from you. Instead, you want to appeal more to the way your cup will make someone feel.

Talking about how someone can feel like a proud mom or feel confident walking into work with a cup that matches their outfit. How much of a compliment it is for someone to ask where you got that tumbler from. How you can show appreciation for your mom, significant other, coworkers, or employees by ordering them a customized tumbler.

Appealing to these types of things will get you sales way more than talking about the features of your cup. People know what a cup does and your cups aren't going to break any records for maintaining ice and that's okay. You can still be very successful by talking to people's emotions, which is what will compel them to buy in the first place.

Create a Website

One of your first orders of business to be successful with selling tumblers is to create a website. Your website will be your main hub for receiving orders and it will help to convey a lot of information to your customers about the products you're offering and what you're capable of making. In addition to these things, a website also helps to build trust with people.

In the modern age, people expect businesses they buy from to have a website and a good-looking website at that. No website at all or a poorly designed website will hurt your sales. Of course, you might be scared of the idea of creating your own website, but you can use a platform such as Wix to easily create your own website using templates.

If you prefer not to go down this route, you can always hire a company or freelancer to create and design your website for you. So what kinds of things should your website offer to visitors? Having a contact me page is an absolute must.

People are going to have questions and if they can't get the answer to their questions by browsing your website, you need to give people a way to reach out to you. Maybe someone is looking for more details on a specific design and they want to see if you'd be able to make it happen for them. Including an about me section is also important because people want to know more about the person who it is they're buying a cup from.

They're not buying a cup from some big company, instead, they're buying a tumbler that's hand-crafted by you. So why not give people some background on who you are, what you like to do in your spare time, and what made you want to start this business in the first place? People getting their questions answered is also huge.

You want to be able to answer common questions on the spot. Sure some people will reach out if they have a specific ask, but other people will be shy and they won't ask you their question. They'll just leave your website never to be seen again.

This is why it's important to have an FAQ page where you can answer some common questions to prevent people from assuming or leaving your website in frustration. The next thing you want to think about is the ordering process. You want to make sure that people have a way to reach out to you if they have a specific request, which we've already covered.

Some people might want something that's more generic. For instance, you could have an order form with drop-down menus that can help someone create their own customized cup. They could choose what color they want their cup to be if they want glitter, and you could even include a box where people could input the text that they want to be on their tumbler, and even upload the photo they want to be used on the cup.

Doing this can help to create a streamlined process for receiving orders for your business. You also want to have plenty of different pictures on your website so that way people can get an idea of what a pink glitter cup would look like for example. You could even put a sample name on there to really give a potential customer a good representation of your designs.

The best way to do this would be to have an image appear when someone selects the color red for instance, an image of one of your red cups would appear so that way people know what they're getting. Then if they switched their answer to blue, a blue cup would appear. Obviously, this is very time-intensive to create, but it's something to think about later on down the line when you're ready to make improvements to your website.

In the beginning though, you definitely want to have pictures of your work on your website so that people can have a good idea of the type of tumbler that you're capable of creating. If you're able to do these things on your website in a way that looks clean, your website will help you make sales. The goal of your website isn't to help make you look flashy, its sole purpose is to help facilitate sales, so keep that in mind.

We Can't Forget About Social Media in Today's Age

Part of being successful with marketing is going where your customers are at. And since pretty much everyone is on social media in the modern age, you're guaranteed to be putting yourself in front of your ideal audience. The mistake that a lot of small business owners make when it comes to social media is that they don't post consistently enough.

They get excited about the idea of creating content to help them drive sales, but then they're never able to post enough for it to actually make a difference. And it makes sense because as a business owner, you have a lot going on. It can also be discouraging to make a post and not see any sales come from it.

The truth is that you have to make a lot of posts consistently for things to gain traction in your business. Make it a goal to build your way to posting once a day on social media. So you might start off with 2 posts per week, then 3, then 5, and then once per day.

The number of platforms you're on is also something to think about. Yes, it makes the most sense to be on every platform, but that's a big bite that most aren't going to be able to swallow on their own unless they have a team helping them.

So only take on as many platforms as you can handle. This will probably be 2-3 at the most, and any platform is good because all of the main ones will have your target audience. So the question really comes down to what should your content be about? Here are some ideas:

Post Every Single Tumbler that You Make

I don't care if you're making a cup for yourself, for a friend for free, for practice, or for a paying customer (with their permission of course), I want you to post every cup that you make. This will do a couple of things for you. The first is it will give off the appearance that you're busy and making sales, which will encourage others to buy from you.

The second is that it will give you a continuous stream of content that you can post. People will get to see the variety of tumblers that you're capable of making. You never know what can come from it.

Someone might see one of your latest creations and think wow I never knew you could make a glitter cup look like that! And now they're a customer all because of a post you made. If you're brand new and you've never made a custom tumbler before, still go ahead and take a picture of it.

If it's a failure, you can post it later on down the line to show people how much you've been able to improve since you first started. People love to follow along with other people's journeys and watch them grow, so this can make for a really powerful post.

Post Videos of You Making Cups

People will be fascinated with watching the process of you making a custom tumbler. The thing is you don't have a make a longer-form video of your process from start to finish. Instead, you can set up different parts of the process across multiple shorter videos.

You could show different styles of tumblers that you make, such as one with glitter, a sublimation tumbler, a tumbler with dye, how you spray paint a tumbler, etc. You could even show the same process using different colors to really give you an endless amount of possibilities. One fear you might have with this type of content specifically is that someone might take your videos and learn the process and do it on their own instead of buying a tumbler from you.

The thing about making custom tumblers though is that it is an artsy project that can get messy and it's a skill. So most people aren't going to want to go through the hassle of buying all of the necessary materials and they're not going to be able to make it look as good as you can. People will enjoy watching these videos though, so it's a great way to get more eyeballs on your page.

Talk About the Different Ways You Can Customize a Tumbler

It's important to share with your audience the different methods and styles you can use to customize a cup because it will help give people an idea of what's possible for you to create for them. So if you're able to use multiple different colors, make a post about that. Make a post talking about how you can add a photo or custom text to a cup to really make it stand out.

If all you post are glitter cups, for example, people will think that's the only thing you're capable of doing. By posting about the different types of possibilities that you are able to create, you can give people an idea of what they'd like to have on their future cup.

What You Love About Making Custom Tumblers

People don't just want to buy a product, they want to buy something from someone who is passionate about what they're doing. So you can create posts where you talk about the joy it gives you to make tumblers and why it makes you happy. It could be that you know your tumblers put smiles on people's faces. You could enjoy the artistic element of the process.

You might love how a custom tumbler is so much more than just a drinking vessel, it's an accessory that you can show off. Whatever your reasons are, be sure to share them with your audience.

Post Polls on Your Stories

A common feature on many social media platforms today is the ability to add pictures and short video clips to your story that will stay up for 24 hours. You can do more than simply post on your story though, you can use things such as polls to help create content that your audience can engage with. One example could be you posting a side-by-side of two different tumblers that you made.

You could then ask the question, "Which design do you think looks better?" People will respond because they'll want to give their feedback. The more people that vote on a poll, the more people who will see the post because this means the post is really engaging.

Not only is this a good way to interact with your audience, but you can also use this to gain good insights into your business. Continuing on with this example, if everyone is only voting for one cup, this tells you that people like that style more, so you should focus more of your efforts on promoting that style of tumbler.

Ask Your Customers to Post Their Cup on Their Profile

Another way that you can take advantage of social media is to ask your customers to post a picture of their cup on their social media profiles and have them tag your account. This will help you to gain exposure to an entirely new audience potentially every time you make a sale. The other thing you could do is take a picture of the cup before you mail it out and tag the customer in the post.

Just make sure you get the customer's permission first. Now it will be easier for the customer to simply share the post to their own story, for example, and you'll still gain the benefit of being exposed to their story all while taking the work off of their plate to post.

Offer Free Giveaways

Another way to make the most of social media is by hosting free giveaways. There are a variety of different ways that you can go about this depending on what you want to achieve. Let's say you go live once a week and you want to increase the number of viewers on your lives.

You could mention in your other posts how you go live every Wednesday at 7pm, and anyone who attends the live will automatically be entered for a chance to win a free customized cup. You could also offer a discount on a cup, the prize you decide to give away is totally up to you. If you want to gain more exposure to your social media page, you can offer to giveaway a free customized cup and to be entered for a chance to win, you must share this post with your followers or you must tag 10 of your friends.

The same thing goes if you want to gain new email subscribers or whatever else the case may be. You can run a contest just because or you can run it because of a holiday coming up, or whatever other reason you can come up with.

Doing this a couple of times per year can work well. If you do it too often, your audience will start to get burnt out on it, but it's still a good tactic to have in your back pocket.

Make Your Own Cup Promoting Your Business

What are some common ways that people promote their business? They might make t-shirts, car decals, koozies, or something else along those lines. These ideas aren't bad, but imagine promoting your custom t-shirt business using a t-shirt.

That would be very specific to what you're doing and people would instantly be able to tell the type of quality that you're capable of producing. If you ran a perfume company and promoted it via a t-shirt, yes this would be effective, but people wouldn't instantly be able to tell how good your perfume is based off of what they can see on the t-shirt. Luckily with a custom tumbler business, you can do the same thing as someone promoting a t-shirt business on an actual t-shirt.

By using a custom tumbler to promote your business, people will instantly be able to see the quality of work that you put out. And since you're going to be carrying your cup with you everywhere you go, it's an easy way to promote your business to anyone you come across without even having to say a word.

This is because your tumbler will do all of the talking for you. Considering that it won't cost you that much to make a cup of your own, you might as well create one solely for the purpose of promoting your company.

Word of Mouth

Having people talk about your cups is a huge way to get more people to buy from you. People trust their friends when it comes to product recommendations. So when someone sees their friend who has a stylish tumbler, they're naturally going to ask where they got it from.

And that person will automatically be trusting of your business because their friend had a good experience with your business. So how do you make word of mouth happen for your business? Well in some ways, you just have to be patient with things.

Word of mouth will naturally start to build as time goes on and you make more sales. However, there are a couple of things you can do to help speed up the process. The first is to make quality tumblers.

If your tumblers aren't inspiring, then people aren't going to want to brag about them to their friends. People aren't going to ask where they got that cup from because they're not going to care.

If you're making quality products, then word of mouth will organically start to happen over time. There is one other thing you can do to start speeding up the process though and that is what I'm about to share with you as my next marketing strategy.

Offer to Make Custom Tumblers for Your Friends and Their Events

If you want to jumpstart the word-of-mouth process, you can do so by offering to make custom tumblers to your friends for free. This especially isn't a bad idea if you're new to making tumblers and you need to get some practice. Obviously, it will be an expense for you to make tumblers for your friends, but you're essentially paying to have your friends market your company for you.

By doing this, you're essentially shortchanging the process of having to build up a customer base that will show off your cups for you. The other thing you can do is offer a discount or potentially even offer to make tumblers for free for your friends' events. So let's say you know of someone who is getting married.

You could offer to make custom tumblers for the bridal party by making wedding-themed cups with each bridesmaid's name on their cup. You could offer to do this at a discount on your normal price since multiple tumblers would be bought, or you could do it for free as more of a promotional type of thing.

Another example of this could be a baby shower. If one of your friends is having a baby, you could give them a custom tumbler with the child's name on the cup or their sonogram picture as part of your gift. Then when the gift is opened everyone will see it and you're getting exposure for your business.

Run Promos for Mother's Day, Father's Day, Around Graduation Etc.

Every year people need to think of a gift to get for their mom or their dad. Additionally, people graduate every year in May. So these are great opportunities to either run a free giveaway or run a promotion that you can talk about on your social media profiles to help increase sales during those times.

For some people, they don't like to have to sit there and think about what gift they want to buy for their mom or dad, so you can come along and take all of the guesswork away from them. If you want, you can even go as far as individually texting friends. Word the message as if it's a group text, but then send it individually to people and you'll be surprised at the response. Here's an example of what you could send:

"Hey ladies! Father's Day is coming up and I'm thinking about running a promo for custom Father's Day tumblers. These tumblers can be made with any type of colors, photos, or text to create a truly one-of-a-kind gift for the special man in your life. I'm going to be giving a good discount on these tumblers from my normal prices, but I'm just trying to see who's interested right now."

Again, a key aspect to this is to make sure that you send this individually to people. If you send it to a big group of people all of whom don't know each other, it's going to be awkward and it's an easy out for no one to respond. By sending it to individuals, it forces people to be more likely to respond.

This message also starts off with a soft ask, you're not asking anyone to commit to buying right now. Instead, you're simply seeing if there's any interest. Sure some people might not respond to the message, but other people will get back to you and say they're interested.

For the people who say they are interested, all you have to do is thank them and say that you'll reach back out with more details later on. After that when the time comes, you can get more details for what they want and then send them a link where they can complete the purchase.

It's important to send out this initial text 2 to 3 months in advance so that you have plenty of time to make the cups and so that people haven't already bought a gift.

Chapter 5: Accomplishing More in Less Time

You may never be interested in bringing on additional help to expand your business. If that's where you're at right now, that's totally okay. You never know, one day though that could change when you find yourself drowning in orders that you can barely keep up with.

Ultimately there will come a time hopefully when your business will be capped with the amount of money that you can make because you can only do so much by yourself, and there's only increasing your pricing up to a certain point. In this chapter, I want to help give you some considerations for when you should bring on an additional person and some things you should look out for.

When Should You Look to Bring on More Help?

It will be awhile before you have to bring on help. Once you're starting to get overwhelmed with orders, your first move should be to look into your pricing and consider increasing it. If you started your business by selling custom tumblers for $30, then by increasing that to $35, you'll be able to make the same amount of money by selling fewer cups.

This will help to take some of the pressure off of you. Your business will continue to grow and soon you'll be selling the same number of tumblers at $35 that you were at $30, so it will again become time to increase your prices once more. Eventually though, you'll reach a ceiling for what the market is willing to pay for a certain item.

Once you reach this ceiling and orders continue to pile in, you're going to need to enlist some additional help. When it comes to being a business owner, there's a lot you have to keep up with. You have to market your business, make the tumblers, and fulfill the order by shipping off the product, not to mention admin type of things like bookkeeping.

So in what aspect of the business should you look to have someone help you out with? Well, it really could be anything. You have to decide what area of the business you think you can gain the most value from someone.

What will save you the most amount of time? In all likelihood, this will be with product fulfillment. Hiring someone to help you make additional tumblers will be the task that will help to save you the most amount of time.

With this though means you'll likely have to train this person on how to make quality custom tumblers. This will take some time, so you'll have to be patient. Of course, there is the possibility that someone might already have experience making tumblers, but depending on who you hire, they might not have any experience.

Let's say though that you want to be solely in charge of making the tumblers, what you could look to do is hire an agency to manage your social media accounts. This way you can be alleviated from some of your marketing duties. Another thing you could look into is hiring a bookkeeper to help you save time in that area of your business.

So there are multiple ways that you can go about things so that you can save time with your business that don't have to involve you hiring an employee. If you are looking to hire someone to help you make tumblers, what are some things that you should consider?

What to Think About When Looking to Bring on Some Additional Help?

Without a doubt, making your first hire is a big decision and it's one that you absolutely want to get right. Hiring the wrong person can set your business way back and cause you to regress. It will make you wish you never hired anyone in the first place.

Hiring the right person though can catapult your business to new heights and save you more time than you ever could have dreamed about. So with that being said, what can you do to ensure you hire the right person? My best piece of advice is to start with people that you already know.

Yes, making custom tumblers is a skill, but it's something that can be taught in a relatively short amount of time compared to other things. It's not like you need to teach someone how to code, for instance. By hiring someone within your network, you can bring someone on who you trust.

You'll know their characteristics and if they'd be a good fit for you. For example, you'd already have a good idea for what their work ethic is like and if you can trust them. If you hire someone you don't know, you have to do your due diligence to ensure you hire the right person, because the last thing you want is to hire someone who steals from your company.

It's easier to hire someone with good characteristics that you can trust and then teach them the skill rather than hiring someone with the skill and having to learn over time if you can trust them or not. Hiring someone outside of your network is also going to cost you money because you're going to need a way for potential applicants to know that you have an opening.

The best way to do this is to use a job board, but these cost money. When it comes to an outside hire, take your time. You don't want to interview one person one time and hire them.

Interview multiple people multiple times and be slow to make your decision because it really is that big of a choice. When deciding who to call for an interview, look at their job history. It doesn't have to be relevant to making tumblers, but that is a plus.

Instead, look and see if they have big job gaps or if they consistently bounce around from one job to the next. You want to interview people who have a steady work history.

You're putting a lot of time and money into hiring someone and training them, so it would be a waste if they leave after 2 months. Once you find a candidate you'd like to interview, start off with a 10-minute phone screen interview.

What to Cover During a 10-Minute Phone Interview

During this interview, you just want to cover basic things such as asking about their work history or any questions you might have based upon their resume, such as why they're looking to leave their current job or what happened at their last job if they're no longer working there.

You also want to cover things that could potentially be deal breakers, such as the number of hours that they'll be working, what their schedule will be, going over what they'll be doing, etc. This way you'll waste as little time as possible just in case someone isn't able to work the schedule you want them to. When conducting this interview, one of the main things that you want to look for is how the person is talking.

Do they sound coherent and confident with what they're saying? Or are they struggling to put sentences together and sound hesitant? If everything checks out, then you can move to an in-person or virtual interview.

What to Cover During the In-Person Interview

With this interview, the main goal is to learn more about them but also see how they would react in certain scenarios. So start off by asking some basic questions such as the following:

- Can you tell me a little bit more about yourself?
- What's your biggest strength?
- What's your biggest weakness?
- What motivates you in the workplace?
- Why do you believe you're the best candidate for this position?

These are all good questions to ask to get a better understanding of the candidate. For example, if they say that their main motivation in the workplace is money, then that could be a red flag because they might not really care to have the attention to detail that would be necessary to succeed in the job.

If someone sounds arrogant with their answer for why they think they're the best candidate, you'll know that if you hire this person, they might be hard to work with. By asking these questions, you'll be able to get a better gauge for the personality of the person and if you would be a good fit for them as a boss. In addition to these questions, you also want to ask some scenario-based questions. Some of the following are some good ideas:

- You're finishing up a tumbler when you drop it and suddenly dents the bottom of it, what do you do?

- You're working on a tumbler when you accidentally knock over a cup of glitter causing it to spill everywhere, what would you do in this scenario?

- You're about to ship off a tumbler to a customer, when preparing for the shipment, you notice the tumbler has a visible scratch on the front of the cup, what do you do?

Questions like these are important to ask because there's a lot that goes into training a new employee. Chances are good that you're going to forget some little detail as to how you'd like things to be done.

So by asking these types of questions, you can see how someone thinks and if they're on the same page as you in regards to how they would handle a certain scenario. If you know how someone would handle a certain situation, then you can feel confident that they would handle other similar scenarios in the same manner.

Conclusion

Starting your own custom tumbler business can be a bit of a mess sometimes just like working with glitter and epoxy can be a bit messy at times. The potential mess is worth it though because this industry is trending in the right direction. There's a lot of money that can be made with this business and you get to have fun creating something unique every time instead of doing the same thing time and time again.

If you're able to follow the advice outlined in this book, I feel confident that you'll be able to see the success that you want to. It's up to you though to be able to execute on the information that you learned and no one else is going to make it happen for you. That's okay though because you cared enough to read this book through to the end, so I believe that you can make it happen!